A Lincolnshire Journey

A Lincolnshire Journey

Stephen Middleton

Illustrations by Polly Welsby.

Matador
9 Priory Business Park
Kibworth Beauchamp
Leicestershire LE8 0RX, UK
Tel: (+44) 116 279 2299
Fax: (+44) 116 279 2277
Email: books@troubador.co.uk
Web: www.troubador.co.uk/matador

ISBN 978-1783062-287

British Library Cataloguing in Publication Data.
A catalogue record for this book is available from the British Library.

Typeset in Aldine by Troubador Publishing Ltd
Printed and bound in the UK by TJ International, Padstow, Cornwall

Matador is an imprint of Troubador Publishing Ltd

With thanks to my father for introducing me to the Lincolnshire countryside all those years ago and to my mother for encouraging my love of books and poetry from an even earlier age.

Grateful thanks also to my erudite young friend and colleague, Ed Turner. Without his professional literary advice and encouragement the Imp would probably not have left the cathedral and certainly would never have travelled so far.

Contents

𝕶oisi

"Koisi" was my name of old. Both young and old am I.

I was old when Paulinus sought my help to bring Christianity to the English.

I was old when the Romans came with their roads and their trade and their wine and their exotic pagan deities.

I was old when men raised stone circles to forgotten gods.

I was born not far from here, a little way along the limestone ridge, in the long Winter when these isles and Europe were one. It was my hunger that hastened the coming of the lush, Holocene Spring. My lust for light and life and warmth and mirth.....

And mischief.

It really was a shame about that window.

It had been Praxiteles' idea, of course, picking the lock on the bishop's wine cellar, but when we got in, honestly, a Sybarite would have blushed. Only that morning the cathedral clergy had been stocking the tithe barns with the harvestings of half-starved, unfree peasants who could barely put a decent meal in the bellies of their scrawny kids. By the time we were on our third bottle of Rhenish, we'd decided that Something Must Be Done.

1

True to form, Praxiteles didn't hang around after we'd had our fun but left me to take the rap. Saint Hugh was furious, despite having passed on his mitre over a century previously and that flaming great swan of his was flapping around threatening to do more damage than *we'd* done. In those days it wasn't enough just to be sorry which I very clearly *was* the following morning with what felt like the clapper from one of the great bells swinging around inside my skull. No. I would just have to do penance.

So, off to Rome on pilgrimage. It was worth the trek though, just to see the look on the Pope's face when I stepped out from the company to kiss the ring. I'll swear his voice jumped three octaves between "pax" and "vobiscum".

They did restore the window eventually. Made a nice job of it actually, beautiful stone tracery, fine as Flanders lace, but that bishop never trusted me again. Hugh stood up for me of course. He never had much time for self-indulgent yes-men. As for that tale about the angel turning me to stone, what utter tosh. I was *born* of the living rock. A useful story for the bishop to put about, no doubt. A warning of the consequences of disobedience.

But make no mistake.

I have stationed myself on high in the cathedral to maintain my vigil.

For I am guardian of my county.

I am the Lincoln Imp.

Cathedral

Through long lancet windows the sun at midday
Lit the floor of the nave with a dappled array
Of multi-hued glory, a fanfare of light,
Reflecting the struggle and triumph of Right.

From over the transept rang out Great Tom's toll
But the peace that ensued was a balm for the soul.
There, allied in defence of their mutual demesne,
The Dean eyed the Bishop, the Bishop the Dean.

But all was not well in the Choir of Saint Hugh
With the new tenor barely recovered from 'flu.
For the poor fellow's "Gloria" grew raucous and pained,
The Precentor's forbearance, increasingly strained.

And the Imp to the seraphim testily snapped
That the "Kyrie Elieson" would p'haps be more apt.
He resolved then to make better use of his day
And after the Eucharist, his fiefdom survey.

So obtaining a nod of assent from Saint Hugh,
Dropping down from his pillar, then dashing on through
The North East transept aisle, he reached the choir screen
(Where he thoughtfully scribbled a note for the Dean).

Then over the nave to the belltower's long climb,
Past stones that were laid in Remigius's time.
Up to the chamber, out into the light,
Shook long-unused feathers, spread his arms and took flight.

Heading into the North at mercurial pace,
Though the radar at Scampton caught barely a trace
Of his flight through the arc of the Lincolnshire sky,
He was vaguely aware of a Presence nearby.

Then all of a sudden, a Damascene light
Hit the Imp and endowed him with strange second sight,
For as he gazed down on the scene there displayed
He seemed to see present and past overlaid.

Over ridged open-fields, slightly dazed, he lost height.
On the branch of a land oak he found some respite
But he knew from their strange, Scandinavian strains
That these sokemen ploughing with oxen were Danes.

The Imp cast a glance up the old Ermine Street,
The cobbles resounding to pounding of feet.
Those troops marching South, he could hear from his perch,
Were complaining in Latin (though Vulgar, not Church).

Flying thoughtfully onwards it seemed to him odd,
Though he'd learned long ago not to argue with God
But at New Holland Pier the truth hit him in full
For the Tattershall Castle was leaving for Hull.

'Midst the flow of the years he was heading upstream
To a place none reclaim save in wish or in dream,
An eldritch-voiced country, uncharted and vast,
Through Time's haunted hinterlands back to the Past.

Time and Tide on the North-East Coast of Lincolnshire

Sea-crafty war smiths,
Shield, helm and ash spear,
Raiding with the East Wind, from the cold North Sea.
Saint Paulinus found them,
Tutored them and tamed them.
Angles into angels on the road to destiny.

Sturdy Danish longships,
Helmed by Grim's own kinsmen,
Sped here by the East Wind, 'cross the cold North Sea.
Their beaten blades with runes adorned,
Their dead in skaldic sagas mourned,
Their place names in the Danelaw like a Viking litany.

Embattled Grimsby trawlers,
Children of the longships,
Battered by the East Wind and the cruel North Sea.
Fish from where their grandsires hailed,
Fish from where the Vikings sailed,
Wrested from the ocean but with bitter penalty.

Steel workers from Rotherham,
Lace makers from Nottingham,
Braced against the East Wind and the cold North Sea.
Briefly freed from factory floor,
No foreman for a week or more,
Sea and sand and Wonderland and fish and chips for tea.

Generations

By the mouth of the Humber, the Lincoln Imp stands
Watching waves of invaders come into his lands.
The county, though torn, was as often as not
Less a cauldron of war, more a deep melting pot

Despite racial tension the young interbred
And Stigand the Saxon took Bronwen to bed.
And Eadred and Ulf were the twins they begat,
Who first farmed the fen, then the Wold after that.
But Ulf's admonitions were uttered in vain,
For Hilda, his child, damn she married a Dane.

Now Snorri the Dane begat Sigbrand and Svart
(Though Hilda, his wife, claimed she too played her part).
And Saxulf the Strong was by Sigbrand begat
And Sigmund the Short was the name of *his* brat,
Who then married a Jute and his own brat begat
(And neither cared much who thought what about that).

When William and Harold had settled their spat,
Then the bloodline of Normandy came with the tide,
But Guy of Warenne took a Saxon for bride.
And they begat Richard and Alais and John
And Robert and Ralf and so on and so on.

Generations of kinsfolk had sprung from the womb.....
But the Imp had lost track of just who begat whom.

In the Blood

From the fjords of the Vestfold or from Alborg's palisade,
Westward sail the war hosts in their panoplies arrayed.
Driven on by lust for plunder or by internecine wars,
The Skagerrak they swiftly cross for Anglo-Saxon shores.
Then the Danegeld's silver harvest they exact from English kings
And the Jarls reward their followers with gifts of golden rings.

Of oak and ash with gilded prows by Viking shipwrights wrought,
By th' East Wind, here, to Lindsey's coast, the dragon
    ships are brought.

The priests upon the Faeroes fled before their tireless tide.
Their merchants sailed the White Sea coast to trade for walrus hide.
To Iceland's cloud-capped peaks they came upon the old ash breeze
And to Greenland sailed their open boats through
    mist-enshrouded seas.
For Vinland's verdant vines they risked the North Atlantic's worst,
John Cabot named it New Found Land but Vikings found it first.

And those who'd raided Lindsey's land now farmed and interbred,
Though lured at first by Lindsey's gold, found Lindsey's maids
instead.

To starboard, dark Icelandic coast, the Straumness Light in view.
The wind whips salt spray from the waves to lash the trawler's crew.
To port, a moving mountain, closing fast through driving sleet
But they climb its trackless slopes and feel it surge beneath their feet.
The swelling sea sweeps inboard as she dips her weather rail,
Then she rolls across to leeward driven by the howling gale
And the halyards' frantic tolling fills the North Atlantic night
And the all-embracing ice reflects the ship's electric light.

The North Wall and the Dock Tower and the taxis to-and-fro
And the smoky New Clee backstreets seem a dream from long ago.

Off Greenland's frozen Cape Farewell the deckies shoot the trawl,
The footrope with its bobbins then the headline, floats and all.
The otter boards pay out behind to hold the trawl net wide,
Then time to haul, off Faeroes Banks or Iceland's bleak West Side.
The jilson lifts the cod ends from the White Sea fishing grounds,
Or maybe fish from Newfoundland lie teeming in the pounds.
The gannets cry their raucous claims amidst the waves' assaults
But below, the silver harvest, safely stowed in ice-clad vaults.

With moonlight on their bow wave, sailing homewards from a shore
Whence their Scandinavian forbears sailed a thousand years before.

If you take the bridge at Fuller Street to view the Humber there,
Or cross the line at Suggitt's Lane to breathe the night sea air,
Does the bittern boom of shipping seem a call from far off lands?
Do you long to stand on distant shores remote
        from Cleethorpes' sands
And like trawler crews see glaciers calve and icebergs floating by
And Northern Lights paint pictures in the cold, clear Northern sky?
If the East Wind brings a wanderlust across the Humber mud
And you dream of far horizons, no surprise, it's in the blood.

Now Grimsby Docks no longer boasts a distant water fleet
And skippers, mates and deckhands drink no more down
    Freeman Street
But though in Riby Square the pubs have long since called,
    "time's up",
They'll drink still in Valhalla, where the ghosts of Vikings sup.

And Odin bids the Valk'ries wake, takes down his golden grail,
Commands the drinking horns be filled, with Hewitt's Premium Ale.

Fish Train

First the whistle's shrilling sound, then a fish train London bound,
Easing through the crossing gates at Cleethorpe Road.
So the traffic has to wait, from the dock to Friargate,
As with syncopated beat, over Holme and Pasture Street,
The locomotive passes slowly with its load.

Whether haddock, cod or skate, on a Royal Doulton plate,
Served with salad and a glass of white Bordeaux,
Or with chips and fried in batter, "Ev'ning Telegraph" for platter.
As your pocket's depth permits, chippie, Corner House or Ritz,
The fish train's calling, be your station high or low.

Now the Imp's astride a buffer, but he's ridden nothing rougher,
Nor for Billingsgate is planning to embark.
So he quits the Gresley mogul just in time to catch a local,
Leaves behind the seagulls' brawling and the trawler sirens calling
And the roaring of the crowd at Blundell Park.

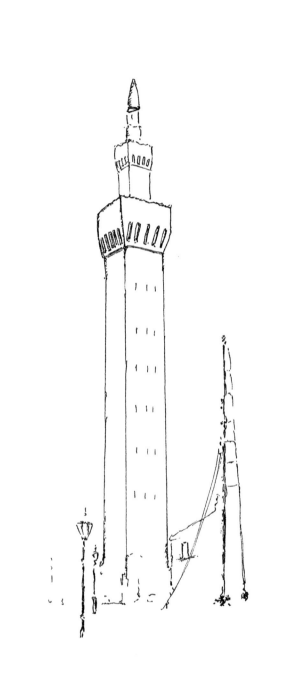

The Great Northern Train

Having started at Grimsby with Firsby its goal,
Passes industries powered by Hewitt's and coal,
Then it clatters past farm over crossing and drain,
Serving fenland and Wold is the Great Northern train.
Weelsby Road, Waltham and Holton-le-Clay,
Then continues cross-country its unswerving way.
Once the road has been set by the North Thoresby box,
Pulls away through a cloud from the cylinder cocks.
Smoke, steam and steel chant a shattering refrain
But the Ludborough station cat yawns his disdain.
Utterby, Fotherby, on to the South
Where the spire of St. James' marks the township of Louth.
Bringing cattlecake, seed and in Summer a group
Clutching buckets and spades for the Mablethorpe loop.
Through stations resembling the farmsteads around,
In red and buff brick with an animal pound.
With mullioned windows and roofs of slate tile,
Domestic Revival, East Lincolnshire style.
But the station at Louth (and some others likewise)
Above the vernacular form seeks to rise
And assumes, with panache, a more elegant air
In mock-Jacobean with fine porte-cochere.
Milk churns to Legbourne and cattle from Authorpe,
Watercress loaded at Aby-for-Claythorpe.
Though Alford and Willoughby near the Wolds stand,
Their livings are bound to the Marsh pastureland.
The fast fitted fish trains flash by for The Smoke
But the slow train's more use to most Lincolnshire folk.

17

The Great Northern it is that the farms here must thank
For the day's pick-up goods and its four-four-two tank.
Gaze far up the line on those timeless hot days,
See the engine take form in the shimmering haze
And the smell of the sleepers comes up with the heat
And life seems to march to a slow exhaust beat.
But now he who patiently waits for a train
At Burgh-le-Marsh, Wragby or Donington-on-Bain
Should know it was here Beeching's Axe did its worst
And he'd likely see Judgement Day pulling in first.

Lincolnshire Roads

We leap o'er dyke and beck and drain,
Bound Tennyson's immortal brook,
Ford Freshney's flow and bridge the Bain,
Then stretch and reach for Donna Nook.

'Round fertile fields we deftly skirt
And scatter tidings on our way.
With Mavis Enderby we flirt
And bid Old Bolingbroke good day.

On Summer days in Wold or fen
For village sounds we gladly pause,
Hear willow crack on leather then,
As wickets fall, genteel applause.

The boundless, endless fen we search,
And quietly cross the hare's domain
To lonely, tree-encompassed church,
An island in this sea of grain.

Now Cadwell's union flag descends
And BSAs with Nortons spar.
Up The Mountain, through Hall Bends
We roar and reek of Castrol "R".

From fitties farms our ways are lined
With saxifrage and meadowsweet.
Now up to Walesby Top we wind
To glint as water in the heat.

At airfield's end we linger now,
But see no more what once we saw.
Cracked runways yield beneath the plough
Which then were England's roads to war.

We race the Lud from out his source
To sylvan vale by Pan endowed.
In truth, from Hubbard's Hills, his course
He holds to flee the strident crowd.

Throughout the marshland day we weave
Past smithy, dairy, church and inn.
This last is blessed by men who leave
What ails without, for ales within.

On Bluestone Heath, from former days,
Just graves remain to tell the tales
Of those who Bronze Age flocks would graze,
Of those who trod our ancient trails.

But are we one or am I we?
For we were one when first were made,
Then burgeoned like a mighty tree
Whose branches spread their welcome shade.

To war's alarms or tyrant's pride
The Lincoln Imp makes swift response.
But even he can't match *our* stride
For we are everywhere at once.

The Road

Aulus Plautius' legions came here by imperial command
Though the world-encircling Ocean filled these seasoned troops
    with dread.
But Necessity and courage brought them safely to this land
And to Lincolnshire it fell to hear the Ninth Hispana's tread.

Then they built their Roman road along the county's limestone spine
Raising forts with bank and rampart where the Corieltauvi dwelt,
And the road brought war; then Samian ware, then honeyed
    Gallic wine
And perhaps it was this latter fare that pacified the Celt.

The "Swan Road", Angles called it, for they came here on the tideway,
From ancestral halls in Jutland to the muddy Humber's mouth.
Then they settled near the Trent and down the old imperial highway,
Royal Lindsey in the county's North and Mercia to the South.

Inside Goltho's timbered hall between the Witham and the Bain,
The ring-thegns at the mead bench swore their fealty to their lord,
But their mettle and their oaths would soon be tested once again
When the Dane sailed up the Humber armed with helm and mail
    and sword.

Walk along the peaceful roads between the Fitties and the fen,
You'll find Conisholme and Grainthorpe, Scandinavian by name.
Nearby Alvingham is English and we know that English men,
Though they paid a Danish taxman, ploughed their furlongs just
 the same.

When a thousand years had passed by since the Ermine Street was
 made,
Then the King's Peace fell upon the road, in Norman William's reign.
For The Conqueror was determined to protect the country's trade
And no-one messed with William, be he Angle, Celt or Dane.

But our medieval roads were not in Roman style constructed,
Nor confined by kerb or hedgerow or by well-trimmed verges bound.
If the road to Market Rasen was by ruts or bog obstructed,
With the blessing of the law, the traveller made a way around.

See how carefully stepped the saltmarsh roads through eerie fret
   and creek
And how gently wound the high Wold ways to ease the oxen's load
And the drovers' flocks, through chalk-flecked vales, their own
   sweet way would seek.
You don't need an English drunk to make a rolling English road.

Such roads as these were mostly by monastic brethren tended
And the uphill drag from Caistor was by Benedictines mended,
Until Henry's Church of England saw such Catholic orders ended
Then the roads went quickly downhill, which, was not what he'd
   intended.

Although turnpikes and enclosures were with tract and shot resisted,
They were needed by the Nation when an Age of Progress came,
But beneath the plough went common land by which the poor
    subsisted,
Little wonder then, in Lincolnshire, a poacher rose to fame.

Once in humble cots of mud-and-stud men rested from their toil
And their smoky village fires were fed from nearby fenland peat,
But the marsh was drained and land reclaimed and new farms
    tilled the soil,
With their seed drills and their horse drawn hoes and all mod
    cons replete.

To serve these Georgian farmsteads, men built many a Georgian mile,
Laying new roads through old open-fields so progress could
    prevail.
Through turnpikes drove both gig and chaise but none could
    match the style
And celerity and glamour of the four-in-hand Louth mail.

(Diversion)

It's The Peacock's cobbled courtyard and a cold and moonlit start,
As the ostler pairs the wheelers so the mail coach can depart,
And the horses' steaming snorts are mingling with the Witham fog,
Then through Holland, with the Stump behind, across the
    fenside bog.

A posthorn's blast at midnight gets the pikegates flung across,
Now a change of horse at Spilsby for the climb to Ulceby Cross,
Then the coachguard checks his hunter and the Mail sets out again,
As the coachman takes the ribbons and the leaders take the strain.

They hold their course for Louth despite the Half Moon's
    homely fare,
Through the earthy smell of cabbages in the chill Autumnal air,
And the silvered clouds are scudding 'cross the silent country night,
And the passengers draw comfort from the coach lamps' feeble light.

On the last descent the coachman slows the coach's quick'ning pace
Lest an axle shear a wheel pin or the horses break a trace,
But the dawn's light finds the Mail safe and each coachman can
    recline
By the fireside with his long clay pipe and glass of hot, spiced wine.

Oh! That such a jewel as this should as a hen house end its days,
Soon outpaced and far outshone by Rail's sublime, ascendant star.
But The Road would soon return to decimate the iron ways,
This time championed by the kin-avenging, furious motor car!

Though The Road ahead seems fraught for you, whichever route
    you take,
And, like Aulus Plautius' legions you forsee your eagles' fall,
Well now, should you lose the highway make the most of your
    mistake,
For in Lincolnshire, the yellow roads are really best of all.

The End of The Road

Gremlins (and other Things that go Bump in the Night)

Somewhere above Lincolnshire, 1944.

(The Gremlins)
We'll cause their glycol tanks to leak
Their leading edge we'll ice.
Now havoc with their course we'll wreak,
'Gainst Death, they'll lose at dice.

Amidst hydraulic pipes we'll dwell,
Their rudder cables grip,
With flaps as well, play merry hell,
No post-op egg this trip.

With flak and fighters we'll collude,
Their wireless set strike dumb
And into Darkie calls intrude
With crackle, hiss and hum.

Although they're on the homeward slog,
The Rhineland well astern,
We'll conjure up a blanket fog
To greet them on return.

For we are gremlins, we infest
Their 'planes and aerodrome.
We'll do our best to send them West
Not Lincolnshire and home.

(The Imp)
I'll keep their mighty merlins sweet,
I'll free their wings from ice.
I'll keep Rolls Royce's jewels in beat
And Death I'll cheat at dice.

Their compass course I'll help maintain,
Through night with danger fraught
And should the gunners peer in vain
I'll yell out "Corkscrew! Port!"

Their wireless set I'll fumigate,
Hydraulic glands keep tight.
I'll see their pilot keeps his date,
They'll prang no kite tonight.

I'll not let gremlins rule the sky
And though they'll jeer and scoff,
The Lincoln Imp am I and I
Will see the buggers off.

In payment of my feudal debt
This sable sky I'll roam.
I'll bring them yet through fog and fret,
To Lincolnshire and home.

30

Et in Arcadia Ego

A sun-warmed nook by heathland fields where Spring wheat
   meets a moss-green gate.
Cow parsley lines the quiet lanes with campion of flame-red hue.
A distant clamour breaks the peace as rooks above their nests
   formate
And though unsighted, sounds of larks descend from out the
   cloudless blue.

Beyond decayed dispersals, near where rusting harrows rest in
   peace,
The old control tower still sees use as nesting martins breed and
   thrive.
The bomb dump serves as playground now, for rabbits bent on
   their increase
And swifts above them climb and turn, then fall in screaming
   power dive.

On first-flown circuits, fledglings, borne above by gentle winds'
   caress,
Reprise the flights once taken here by larger and more deadly kin.
The sound of raucous laughter loudly echoes near the crumbling
   mess,
As there the jackdaws, drunk on life, reprise the songs of those
   within.

Bloodied but unvanquished sons, here vectored by cathedral
  towers,
From city smoke or gentle shires or yet from distant lands were
  sprung.
What Winter takes, the Earth remakes, as Spring arrives 'midst
  sun-wreathed flowers.
Don't search for old ghosts in this place, for here you'll only find
  the young.

A sun-warmed nook by heathland fields where Spring wheat
  meets a moss-green gate.
Cow parsley lines the quiet lanes with campion of flame-red hue.
A distant clamour breaks the peace as rooks above their nests
  formate
And though unsighted, sounds of larks descend from out the
  cloudless blue.

Incident at St Gertrude's

Stragglethorpe, Theddlethorpe, Stainton-le-Vale,
Kirkby-cum-Osgodby, Newton-by-Toft.
Welton-le-Wold, Little Cawthorpe, Great Hale,
Haceby and Braceby and Laceby and Croft.

St Luke's and St Anne's, high in chalk-marbled vales,
Keep close watch and ward on the welfare of men.
St John's and St Mark's weather History's gales.
Like tall ships at anchor they lie in the fen.

But follow the drove road past Wodenby Farm,
To churchyard revetted with cedars and yews
And enter St Gertrude's, an enclave of calm.
Draw strength, as do all those who rest in these pews.

Late Norman the nave, Early English the tower,
Octagonal pulpit with eagle of brass,
A fine turret clock striking each quarter-hour,
Ornate tie-beam roof and Victorian glass.

Now one Friday evening some Summers ago,
Mrs Timms was alone with her floral display.
The church seemed alive in the roseate glow
When clear from the chancel came sounds of affray.

For the Lincoln Imp sat there in heated debate
With a cat with green eyes and with fur black as night
And the pair were contesting if sin was innate
Or result of contemporary concepts of right.

34

Disputing theology, ethics and law,
Each other's convictions they trampled roughshod.
The cat probed for weaknesses, seeking a flaw
In the arguments reckoned to verify God.

What god, asked the cat, would permit Man his wars?
And the Imp, for a moment, was on the back hoof,
But his Causal Hypothesis gave the cat pause,
Though he wasn't prepared to accept it as proof.

The cat quoted Nietzsche and Kant for a start,
Then dwelt on Empirical Truth for a spell.
The Imp drew (in part) upon René Descartes
And Aristotelian logic as well.

They argued Ontology pillar to post,
Toward Teleology started to veer
But the question that bothered the both of them most
Was could England recover The Ashes that year?

Then equal on points and with honour intact,
The Imp and the cat both departed to dine.
Mrs Timms wasn't sure how she ought to react....
But she quietly replaced the communion wine.

Now those who find rambling a blesséd release
And rest in St James' or St John's on their way,
Care much for their ancientry, beauty and peace
But little for what cats *or* imps have to say.

Bilsby and Bolingbroke (both New and Old),
Deeping St Nicholas, Grainthorpe and Lea.
Farforth-cum-Maidenwell, Gayton-le-Wold,
Croxby and Roxby and Sutton-on-Sea.

Wayward and the Windmill Cat

Victoria's portrait hangs on schoolroom walls
From Kensington to Karekare Falls.
Her Peoples, jew'ls in her imperial crown
And from an English heaven, God smiles down.
At sea, the Pax Britannica holds sway
With Mons and Ypres fifteen years away.
A lonely outpost, now, this empire holds
In Lincolnshire, high on the Eastern Wolds.
Here lives a green-eyed tabby, apt to roam,
And bring anxiety to loving home.
This cat, of misdemeanours unashamed,
So wayward is, and so, is "Wayward" named.

The Devil's promptings Wayward never knew
But curiosity will often do
To drive a little cat to wander so
And far from farm and friendly fireside go.

That Christmastide, a hoar frost on the ground,
This brindled pilgrim for The Marsh is bound,
Throughout the night, from out the Wold,
To seek the fairest thing, so he's been told.
A windmill! Sail and crank and iron rod,
Devised by mind of Man but turned by God.

(Song of the Winter Night)
> *Frosted, moonlit track discerning,*
> *Friends and fire and hearth rug spurning,*
> *Through the furze and heather crawling,*
> *Startled by the barn owl's calling.*
>
> *Over frozen puddles skating,*
> *Chalkland pathways navigating,*
> *Into drainage ditches stumbling,*
> *Through the darkened hedgerows fumbling.*
>
> *Passage through a farmyard seeking,*
> *Past the pullets, havoc wreaking,*
> *Gingerly, 'round kennels veering,*
> *Destination now he's nearing.*

The dawn at last reveals his glitt'ring prize
And, tail held high, the last few miles he flies
To township's edge, hard by the pasturelands.
It's here, before the windmill, rapt, he stands.
An ogee cap atop the tarred black tower,
With patent sails to tap the East Wind's power.
But suddenly, its doors swing open wide.
Out steps a ghost-white cat with warlike stride.
With hissing, bristling fur and backs arched 'round,
This tense, unyielding pair defend their ground.
The Sundance Kid or Wyatt Earp stood so
And Davy Crockett at the Alamo.
The townsmen urge their womenfolk inside
And doors and shutters slam lest woe betide.

Although mid-morn it feels more like High Noon,
But parity compels a change of tune,
For, feigning unconcern, the two at length,
Content with their respective shows of strength,
Touch noses and agree an end to war
And life resumes its sleepy pace once more.

Now "Gladstone" was the mill cat's given name
In memory of the Grand Old Man's acclaim
And whilst his spectral pallor seemed a fright,
Beneath the flour, his fur was black as night.
He proved an educated kind of cat
And systematic in pursuit of rat.
He scorned all those who, learning, thought uncool,
For Gladstone had attended grammar school.
Soliloquies from "Hamlet" he'd relate
And even Latin verbs would conjugate.
He planned to beat the Boer at chess and bring
An ending to the siege of Mafeking.
Though doubtful of a farm cat's grasp of gears,
A mill tour he suggests, despite his fears.
Didactic and declaiming he may be,
Yet Wayward greets this with alacrity.
He's steered (though under guidance, he'll allow)
A Ruston Proctor steam-hauled balance plough,
So knows he's little cause to be afraid
Of gadgets dating from the Third Crusade.

(Song of the East Wind)

> Shuttered sails for East Wind yearning,
> Windshaft, brake- and crownwheel turning,
> Through the trapdoors, sack hoist hauling,
> Harvest from the grain bins falling.
>
> Spurwheel, stone nuts, quant rotating,
> Height of stones self-regulating,
> Wheat grain from the feed shoe tumbling,
> Stones of Paris quartzite rumbling.
>
> Timbers, like a tall ship's, creaking,
> Windmill to the miller speaking,
> Sail and cog and shaft and gearing,
> Masterpiece of engineering.

Between the fantail and the loading stage,
All day, in discourse, these two friends engage.
Home Rule divides the pair, in tense debate.
Free Trade, however, both cats deprecate.
But as the sinking sun foretokens freezing night,
The news has reached the town of Wayward's flight.
He's gently lifted to the miller's cart
And Gladstone, sadly, sees his friend depart
Past timbered mews, through gaslit, Georgian street,
With politics and mills at last replete.

The cheery carter, from his hearty song,
Had drunk of Bateman's Bitter far too long.
His stalwart shire, however, Wayward knew,
By luck, was Nonconformist through and through
And never, ever drank would you believe
(Save p'haps a glass of port on Christmas Eve).

The wind has lightened, shuttered sails are still,
As cat and cart wind up the Westward hill
And head on high into the darkened Wold.
Then Wayward, huddled 'gainst the growing cold
Looks back and is enchanted by the sight,
Illumined by the moon's ethereal light.

The windmill and St Gertrude's tower likewise,
Above an overlying ground fog rise.
All else of Man beneath the star-strewn skies,
His frosted fields, his farmsteads, hidden lies,
Save here and there where darker, rising cloud,
A homely hearthfire marks, beneath the shroud.

Amidst the hessian smell and bags of flour,
Through gathering cloud, hour after lonely hour.
This change, it seems, presages Winter snows
But now a gate that Wayward's sure he knows
And as the first fat flakes begin to fall,
With practised ease he leaps the farmyard wall.
Then noses through the open scullery door,
Runs past the copper, 'cross the stone-flagged floor.
Accepts the maid's rebukes with guileless face,
But bits of ham with rather better grace.
The inner cat, with gusto, he restores.
To aspidistra'd parlour then withdraws.
The longcase clock taps out its gentle beat
As Wayward dozes with the hearthfire's heat.
A token wash, no more, then green eyes close.
On, through the night, in undisturbed repose.

Snow reflects the lantern's gleaming,
By the fire a cat lies dreaming.

(The Night)   *Frosted, moonlit track discerning,*
(The Wind)   *Shuttered sails for East Wind yearning,*

	Friends and fire and hearthrug spurning,
(The Night)	Friends and fire and hearthrug spurning,
(The Wind)	Windshaft, brake- and crownwheel turning,
(Etc.)	Through the furze and heather crawling,
	Through the trap doors, sack hoist hauling,
	Startled by the barn owl's calling,
	Harvest from the grain bins falling.
	Over frozen puddles skating,
	Spurwheel, stone nuts, quant rotating,
	Chalkland pathways navigating,
	Height of stones self-regulating,
	Into drainage ditches stumbling,
	Wheat grain from the grain bins tumbling,
	Through the darkened hedgerows fumbling,
	Stones of Paris quartzite rumbling.
	Passage through a farmyard seeking,
	Timbers, like a tall ship's, creaking,
	Past the pullets, havoc wreaking,
	Windmill to the miller speaking,
(The Night)	Gingerly, 'round kennels veering,
(The Wind)	Sail and cog and shaft and gearing,
(The Night)	Destination now he's nearing,
(The Wind)	Masterpiece of engineering.

Snow reflects the lantern's gleaming,
By the fire a cat lies dreaming.

Requiescat.

Evensong

From Humber to Wash and through each wapentake,
From the old Pax Romana to the EU mistake,
The Imp ranged all day, but as shadows grew long
His view of the past seemed at last to be gone.

By the Blue Stone Heath Road, heading homewards at last,
From Calceby's sad stones up to Stenigot's mast,
Crossing over the Bain t'wards the Westering glow,
Intending to follow the Witham's broad flow.

He could see, flying low over reedbed and sedge,
The cathedral stand proud on the high Lincoln Edge.
Over fenland and delph, under darkening sky,
Then the still distant bells pealed a welcoming cry.

Well aware of the closeness of Waddington's base,
Not daring to trespass inside their airspace,
He kept well to the North so as not to encroach
As he lined himself up for his final approach.

For past misdemeanours he'd made full amends.
Now the Imp and Saint Hugh were the firmest of friends.
To Hugh's pinnacled statue he soon made his way
And the pair watched together the embers of day.

In his Angel Choir home he regained his old seat,
Thinking Evensong's strains never sounded so sweet.
Though his mind was still full with his tour of his fief
He was sure that he'd caught the Dean's sigh of relief.

And the Imp then reflected on where he had been,
And how Time had brought change to the Lincolnshire scene.
He'd watched acres of marshland turned fertile and green,
And the story of farming unfold.

Though far fewer windmills tower over the land,
The East Wind's still harnessed by Man's skilful hand,
And Lincolnshire's churches like sentinels stand,
Vigilant, ageless and bold.

He'd seen races arrive here to pillage and kill,
Now the children of all plough the Lincolnshire till,
And their grandsires and grandams lie sleeping here still,
Deep in the heart of the Wold.

The "Magnificat" swelled forth both pure and sublime,
The new tênor well dosed with honey and lime.
"Qui cantat, bis orat" Augustine once told,
The Precentor's delight now a sight to behold.

Epilogue

And near Kirkby-with-Muckby-cum-Sparrowby-cum-Spinx,
In Betjeman's Tale of the County of Lincs.,
The tenantless acres stay eerie and fell
And the Speckleby rector still tolls on his bell.

Glossary

Alborg – Now an industrial city in North East Denmark. Archaeological excavation indicates that this was originally a fortified settlement.

"Angles into angels" – A pun first used by Gregory I (Pope AD 590 – 604) who, on seeing two English boys in a slave market and concerned over the institution of slavery, observed that they were "Non Angli sed angeli", (not Angles but angels).

Ash breeze – Oars were made from white ash wood. "The ash breeze" is a phrase used even today to mean rowing.

Ashes – The Imp and the cat's debate clearly has echoes of that recorded in the *Wipers Times*, the First World War soldiers' newspaper ("Wipers" being the soldiers' rendition of "Ypres"). Whilst mud and military matters featured highly among their concerns, their main obsession was "whether Notts County could beat Aston Villa." The Imp and the cat may have had rather more sophisticated sporting concerns but obviously a sense of proportion was evident in both conflicts.

Aristotelian logic – A formalised, deductive method of logic. (Aristotle 384-322BC.)

Aulus Plautius – Appointed by the Emperor Claudius to command the invasion of Britain in AD 43. He had four legions, the IX Hispana, the XX Valeria Victrix, the II Augusta and the XIV Gemina. His army initially mutinied at the prospect of crossing the "Ocean" and fighting in unknown lands.

Bain – River

Batemans – Brewery founded in Wainfleet in 1874 and still supplying "Good, Honest Ales" to Lincolnshire pubs.

Brakewheel – Large gear wheel mounted on the windshaft in a windmill.

Beeching – Dr Beeching was responsible for the closure of 25% of Britain's railways in the years immediately after 1963. In truth, he seems to have accelerated a process that had already been underway for some time. The Bardney to Louth line, which included Wragby and Donington-on-Bain, finally closed in 1960, some time before Beeching started to swing his axe.

Billingsgate – London fish market.

Bishop's Eye – There are two beautiful rose windows at either end of the cathedral transept known as The Bishop's Eye and The Dean's Eye. The Dean's Eye dates from the rebuilding period after the earthquake of 1185. The original Bishop's Eye was also from this period but was rebuilt around 1330. According to the Imp's account he seems to have been the reason for this.

Cabot, John – Late 15th century explorer sponsored by Henry VII.

Castrol R – Lubricating oil derived from the castor bean (hence, originally, "Castrol"). It was used for racing engines and you'll mostly find it these days at Classic events. It smells...just...gorgeous.

Cathedral towers – Aircrews returning from bombing missions used Lincoln Cathedral as a landmark to help them navigate back to their bases.

Calceby – St Andrew's Church. Very little of the original medieval structure survives.

Chaise – Horse drawn vehicle.

Chamber – The bell chamber where the ringers pull the bell ropes.

Cod ends – The final section of the trawl net in which the fish are held.

Corieltauvi – The British tribe which occupied the area when the Romans arrived.

Corkscrew – Evasive manoeuvre.

Crownwheel – The gear wheel at the top of a windmill with upwards pointing teeth.

Danegeld – A tax on the English to provide payment for the Danes to prevent them from pillaging and which was usually paid in the form of silver coinage. The Danes were effectively running a sort of protection racket.

Danelaw – The area of Eastern England settled by the Vikings (in which Danish law ran).

Darkie – Codeword transmitted by an aircraft in distress.

Dean's Eye – See Bishop's Eye.

Deckies – Deckhands.

Delph – A local name for a drainage ditch.

Descartes, René – 17th Century philosopher who famously stated, "I think, therefore I am". His religious beliefs have been variously interpreted, although he claimed his *Meditations* were written in defence of religion.

Domestic Revival – Architectural offshoot of the Arts and Crafts Movement, mid-19th Century, also known as "Old English Style".

Eagles – The legions' standards, loss of which was synonymous with defeat.

East Wind – The cold East Wind is a constant feature of life on or near the East coast of Lincolnshire. Interestingly, the East Wind seems to have an evil reputation in several literary and historical traditions. It is harvested these days by numerous wind farms.

Et in Arcadia Ego – From the title of Poussin's famous painting, the implication being "Even in this idyll, I, Death, am here". Fifty-five thousand members of Bomber Command died between 1939 and 1945. In age, most were late teens to early twenties. Lincolnshire is littered with the remains of bomber airfields.

Ermine Street – Roman Road, now the A15.

Fantail – Small, wind-powered fan mounted on the back of the windmill's cap which keeps the sails pointed into wind.

Feudalism – Generally regarded as a system whereby a fief (land or sometimes property) was granted to a vassal by an overlord in return for allegiance and service which would often, but not always, be military in nature.

Fief – see Feudalism.

Fitties – Salt marsh.

Footrope/Headline – These form the mouth of the trawl net.

*Four-four-two tan*k – The C12 tank engine, designed by H.A. Ivatt, which was used extensively in Lincolnshire from the 1920s to the late 1950s. It had four leading, four driving and two trailing wheels.

Four-in-hand – Four horses controlled by one coachman as with a stagecoach.

Free Trade – In the last quarter of the 19th Century, Britain reduced the tariffs on imported goods, encouraging other countries to do the same. This resulted in a flourishing market for Britain's industries but led to a flood of cheap, imported corn, especially from America.

Fret – Local name for a sea mist which drifts inland.

Gig – Horse drawn vehicle.

Gladstone – William Ewart Gladstone was British Prime
    Minister four times during the Nineteenth Century. A
    major social and electoral reformer, *The Times* referred to
    him as "G.O.M.", the "Grand Old Man". He died in
    1898.

Gloria – "Gloria in Excelsis Deo". Latin. "Glory be to God in
    Heaven". One of the canticles from the Eucharist.

Glycol – Engine coolant.

Great Tom – Lincoln Cathedral's largest bell, housed in the
    central tower.

Gremlins – Perhaps a species of goblin but one that seems to
    have evolved specifically to live on RAF aircraft. Earliest
    documentary references date to the 1920s and RAF
    training manuals attest to the many forms of sabotage of
    which they were capable.

Gresley mogul – Sir Nigel Gresley was Chief Mechanical
    Engineer for the Great Northern Railway from 1911, then
    after Grouping in 1923, the London and North Eastern
    Railway, until his death in 1941. A mogul is a locomotive
    with two leading and six coupled driving wheels. The one
    the Imp hitched a ride on was probably a K2 or a K3.

Grim – The 13th Century tale of *Havelok the Dane* records that
    Grim was the founder of Grimsby. Some postulate that,
    despite Grim's Danish origins, this took place before the
    main period of Viking invasions. There are, perhaps, more
    convincing explanations for the derivation of the name of
    the town.

Hewitts – Grimsby brewery, finally closed in 1968 after a century of brewing beer for the local area.

Holland – The Southernmost of the three medieval "Parts" or divisions of Lincolnshire, the other two being Lindsey and Kesteven.

Holocene – The post-glacial period which began c.10,000 years ago.

Home Rule – Gladstone's last political act before resigning as prime minister in 1894 was to attempt to pass a bill giving home rule to Ireland. He failed.

Hubbard's Hills – Beauty spot near Louth. Beautiful indeed, though often crowded.

Hunter – Pocket watch with a protective, hinged lid.

Invasions – Genetic, linguistic and archaeological studies have led to the overthrow of the Invasion Hypothesis which saw large numbers of invaders arriving in successive waves throughout prehistory and into historical times with consequent radical linguistic, cultural and population changes. Modern research suggests that, even when such invasions are historically attested, they involved relatively small numbers of individuals. Greater credence is now given to the idea that linguistic and cultural change may have been brought about through indigenous development and by the influence of small numbers of incomers establishing themselves as ruling elites. The Imp may well have stood by the mouth of the Humber and watched "waves of invaders" but they were probably quite small waves.

Jarl – Related to Anglo-Saxon "eorl" or "earl". A high ranking Scandinavian noble.

Jilson – The large hook and hawser used to raise the "bag" of fish.

Kant, Immanuel – 18th Century philosopher. Not necessarily hostile to religion, Kant was certainly critical of some of the traditional arguments for belief in God and of the role of Christianity.

Kirkby with Muckby etc. – An acknowledgement of the inspiration I have derived from Betjeman's poem, *A Lincolnshire Tale*, which beautifully evokes the spirit of the county. Kirkby etc., is a mythical place near which is the desolate village of Speckleby, inhabited only by the ghostly rector.

Kin-avenging, furious… – A reference to the Erynes, the "kin-avenging furies" of Greek myth.

Kyrie Eleison – Canticle from the Eucharist sung as an alternative to the "Gloria", especially during Lent. Greek. "Lord have mercy upon us", which is possibly what the Imp was thinking.

Lancet windows – The cathedral nave's windows which depict stories from the gospels in stained glass.

Leaders – The two leading horses of a stagecoach.

Lincoln Imp – (See also "Bishops Eye" and "St Hugh".) The Lincoln Imp is a twelve-inch high, stone creature sitting on one of the columns in the Angel Choir in Lincoln

Cathedral. Popular mythology, purportedly dating from the 14th century, states that two such creatures flew in and vandalised the cathedral one night as well as tripping up the bishop. An angel appeared out of a hymn book and turned the more aggressive imp to stone. A similar fate is reported to have befallen the second imp but not before he had taken up residence in St James' church in Grimsby.

Now you know the truth.

The Imp's account at the beginning of this collection leaves it open to question as to which bishop he upset but given the fact that the rose window known as The Bishop's Eye had to be rebuilt in 1330, it was possibly Henry Burghersh. He had a somewhat chequered career, joining the faction which removed Edward II and later supporting Edward III. He suffered a term of imprisonment and seems to have had a reputation for oppressing the poor.

It seems remotely possible that the Imp's name for himself (Koisi) was his original birth name. The University of Wales' Centre for Advanced Celtic and Welsh Studies has produced a vocabulary for a proto-Celtic language, reconstructed through comparative linguistics. The word "Koisi" is listed and translates as "guardian". (The final "i" of his name may have originally been a stem ending rather than a suffix.) Some authorities propose considerable antiquity for this language. Palaeolithic Continuity Theory (though it has few adherents) sees a proto-Indo-European language dating back even to the Palaeolithic.

I can infer little concerning the name of the other imp,

Praxiteles. He may have been named or nick-named after the 4th Century BC Athenian sculptor but whether that was in recognition of the imp's statuesque appearance or as a consequence of the sculptor's alleged obsession with the female form is unknown.

Lindsey – Anglo-Saxon kingdom. Later, one of the three "Parts" of Lincolnshire. See Holland.

Lud – The river which runs through Hubbard's Hills

Mafeking – The Siege of Mafeking and its relief were among the most famous incidents of the Boer War. Mafeking was under siege by the Boer forces between October 1899 and May 1900, a total of 217 days.

Magnificat – One of the canticles from Evensong, the Virgin Mary's hymn of praise. Latin. "Magnificat anima mea Dominum." "My soul magnifies the Lord."

Marsh – The rich, pastoral area between the Wolds and the sea.

Mons and Ypres – Two of the opening, bloody conflicts of the First World War.

Mercia – Anglo-Saxon kingdom.

Merlins – Aero engines. The Merlin was Rolls Royce's masterpiece which powered a range of aircraft from Spitfires to Lancasters.

Mess – Aircrew dining area and bar and a place for crews to let off steam.

Mud-and-stud – Construction technique similar to wattle and daub but more economical of wood and virtually unique to Lincolnshire.

Nietzsche, Friedrich – 19th Century philosopher who famously pronounced, "God is dead".

Ninth Hispana – The famous *Legion of the Ninth* of Rosemary Sutcliffe's novel. It seems to have picked up its Spanish title as a result of the Romans' campaigns against the Cantabrians. It was responsible for the conquest of Eastern Britain, pushing up along the line of what became the Ermine Street to Lincoln. Its later fate is uncertain, though there are a number of scholarly hypotheses.

North Thoresby box – "The road" is the railwayman's term for the line. "Setting the road" means the signal box has set signals and points in the train's favour.

North Wall – The part of Grimsby docks against which trawlers ready to leave were drawn up.

Ogee cap – The onion-shaped cap which characterises Lincolnshire's tower windmills.

Ontology – That branch of philosophy which considers the nature of existence.

Open fields – Medieval farming method whereby fields are unbounded by hedges or fences and divided into long, cambered strips or "lonts". These can be seen today in the form of corrugations in the landscape.

Ostler – In charge of the horses.

Patent sails – Windmill sails with a shutter system (a little like a venetian blind) which allows the speed of rotation to be controlled.

Pax Britannica – The peace imposed by the Royal Navy throughout the Nineteenth Century, c.f. Pax Romana.

Pax Romana – The peace imposed by the Roman legions.

Pax vobiscum – Latin. "Peace be unto you".

Peacock – In the 18th Century, The Peacock was a large coaching inn at Boston.

Poacher – *The Lincolnshire Poacher*. Written 1757, it has become the county's theme song.

Port-cochere – An elaborate covered entrance originally designed to allow well-to-do- passengers to alight from a coach.

Post-op egg – Eggs were strictly rationed during the Second World War. On a bomber base, the pre- and post-operation egg was a privilege accorded only to aircrew.

Praxiteles – (*Prax-it-el-ees*) See Lincoln Imp.

Precentor – In charge of the music in a cathedral.

Quant – Drive shaft in a windmill.

Qui cantat bis orat – Latin. "He who sings prays twice".

Remigius – Founded the Cathedral in the time of William the Conqueror.

Requiescat – A terrible old pun but irresistible. Latin. "He rests."

Ribbons – 18th century term for reins.

Ruston Proctor balance plough – Rustons was an engineering firm founded in Lincoln in 1840. Through various name changes, mergers and takeovers it survives to this day. A balance plough was hauled backwards and forwards across the field by two traction engines which were positioned at the field sides. It is more likely that, by the end of the 19th Century, Wayward's farm would have been using the more advanced anti-balance plough but I can justify the former over the latter on two counts:-
      1/ It seems unlikely that a cat with Wayward's reputation would have been entrusted with the most up-to-date machinery.
      2/ It wouldn't scan.

Sagas – Scandinavian chronicles. Grimsby is actually mentioned in the *Orkneyinga Saga*, though it is not a particularly flattering portrait.

Samian Ware – Red-glazed pottery produced in Italy and Gaul and exported throughout the Roman Empire.

Scampton – RAF base just North of Lincoln. The famous Dambuster Raid was flown from here.

Skagerrak – The sea between Norway and Denmark.

Skald – Scandinavian bard.

Seraphim – The highest in the Judeo-Christian tradition's hierarchy of angels.

Sokemen – (*soke-e-men*) Scandinavian equivalent of the medieval villein and found mainly in Eastern England. A peasant farmer but one free of obligation to a lord.

Spurwheel – The largest gear wheel in a windmill.

Straumness – (More correctly, "Straumnes".) Lighthouse on extreme North West tip of Iceland. The third verse of "In the Blood" was inspired by and partly based on Chris Nicklin's account of the night the trawler *Thuringia* nearly turned over in a storm under the weight of ice. If you think my description sounds hair raising, you should read his.

Stenigot – Surviving World War Two radar tower.

Stone nuts – Small gearwheels in a windmill which drive the runner stones.

Stump – "The Stump" is the local name for St Botolph's church tower which can be seen for miles across the South Lincolnshire flatlands.

St Gertrude's – You will search Lincolnshire in vain for this church. St Gertrude is the patron saint of cats.

St Hugh – The 12th Century saint closely associated with Lincoln Cathedral. He was responsible for initiating the rebuilding of the cathedral after the earthquake of 1185. He seems to have been a formidable and admirable character, generous to the poor and unafraid of rebuking the Angevin kings, Henry II and his son Richard I (Cour de Lion) whilst defusing their anger with humour. King John he seems to have regarded as beneath contempt. He is always associated with his pet swan which was said to be fiercely loyal to him. His carved figure above the Langford Manor stall in St Hugh's Choir in the cathedral shows him with this swan. He died in 1200 and was canonised in 1220.

St Paulinus – Credited with converting the Anglo-Saxon kingdom of Lindsey to Christianity in the 620s. He founded a church at Lincoln at the request of Bleacca, the city's praefectus.

Tattershall Castle – One of the ferries which sailed across the Humber until the Humber Bridge opened in 1976 and now a floating restaurant on the Thames.

Teleology – That branch of philosophy which considers that intelligent design may play a role in the nature of the universe.

Thegn – Variously spelled "thegn", "thane" or "theyn". In Anglo-Saxon England, he was the personal retainer of a lord to whom he swore fealty and from whom he received land in return for military service. Gifts of rings would be given by the lord as tokens of the bond. In the great Anglo-Saxon poem, *Beowulf*, the term "Ring-Danes" is used and this bond, of course, forms the basis for Professor JRR Tolkien's book, *The Lord of the Rings*.

Third Crusade – Most historians are of the opinion that windmills were introduced into Europe as a result of contact with the Saracen forces during the Third Crusade, 1189-92.

Tract – Political pamphlets common in 18th century.

Valkeries – Old Norse. "Those who choose the slain". Fearsome female deities responsible for bearing the bodies of warriors fallen in battle to Valhalla.

Valhalla – Old Norse. "The halls of the slain", where the chief Scandinavian god, Odin, gathers those warriors who have fallen in battle. *The Poetic Edda*, the main source for these myths, refers to mead being drunk, however, rather than ale.

Vestfold – South East Norway.

Vernacular – The architecture of ordinary buildings.

Vulgar Latin – The Latin which would have been spoken by ordinary Romans as opposed to Church Latin which is an elevated, formalised language.

Waddington – RAF base to South East of Lincoln.

Wapentake – A division of the Danelaw. Lincolnshire was divided into thirty-three wapentakes which were still used as administrative areas as late as the 19th Century. They were Eastern England's equivalents of the hundreds and their name (Old Norse, "vapnatak", "weapon-taking") is likely to have derived from their use as military units.

West – as in "to go West", a euphemism for death.

Wheelers – The two horses closest to the coach which had to be matched for length of stride.

Windshaft – The shaft which carries the sails in a windmill.

Witham – River.

Wonderland – Funfair and amusements on the sea front at
  Cleethorpes, built in 1911.

Yellow roads – In Ordnance Survey maps, unclassified or
  minor roads are coloured yellow.

Ypres – See Mons

Select bibliography

Whilst *A Lincolnshire Journey* doesn't pretend to be a serious academic excursion it is certainly grounded in a desire for historical, technical and geographical accuracy. I have found the following useful as sources of information and, on occasion, inspiration.

Sir W.Addison, *The Old Roads of England*, Batsford, 1980.

P.Anderson, *Lincolnshire Railway Memories*, Irwell Press, 2007.

J.Arnold, *All Drawn by Horses,* David and Charles, 1979.

R.W.Bagshawe, *Roman Roads*, Shire, 1972.

Bede, *Ecclesiastical History of the English Speaking People.* (L.Sherley-Price transl.) Penguin, revised 1990.

S.Bennett, *A History of Lincolnshire*, Phillimore, 1970.

K.Cameron, *English Place Names*, Bastsford Books, 1996.

R.Chartrand, K.Durham, M.Harrison and I.Heath, *The Vikings*, Osprey, 2006.

J.R. Clarke-Hall (transl.) *Beowulf,* Allen and Unwin, revised 1950.

G.J. Crossland and C.E. Turner, *Great Grimsby. A History of the Commercial Port*, T and C Publishing, 2002.

D.Cuppleditch, *The Lincolnshire Coast*, Sutton Publishing Ltd., 1996.

D.Cuppleditch, *The Lincolnshire Wolds*, Sutton publishing Ltd., 1997.

J.Currie, *Lancaster Target*, Goodall Publication, 1977.

C.Dickens, *The Pickwick Papers*, Everyman's Library, 1997 (first pub. 1837).

P.Dolmer, *Lincolnshire Windmills: a contemporary survey*, Lincolnshire County Council, 1986.

C.Ekberg, *Grimsby Fish*, Barracuda Books, 1984.

S.Frere, *Britannia:A history of Roman Britain*, Routledge and Keegan Paul, 1987.

A.Hallett, *Markets and Marketplaces of Britain*, Shire, 2009.

J.Harries, *Discovering Churches*, Shire, 1972.

P.Hartshorne, (Ed.) *Lincoln Cathedral: A Journey from Past to Present*, Third Millenium Publishing, 2011.

B.P.Hindle, *Medieval Roads*, Shire, 1982.

J.Hospers, *An Introduction to Philosophical Analysis*, Routledge, 1956.

H.C.Hutson, *Sparks around the Bridge*, North-East Lincolnshire Council Museum Services, 1996.

D.Jager, *Windmills of Lincolnshire Surviving into the Twentieth Century*, Heritage Lincolnshire, 2007.

P.K.King and D.R.Hewings, *The Railways around Grimsby, Cleethorpes, Immingham and North-East Lincolnshire,* Foxline Publishing, 1988.

G.Larn, *Beer, Hope and Charity*, Century Zero Four Publications, 2008.

Lincoln Cathedral. The Story So Far. (Uncredited) Lincoln Minster Shops publ., 2006.

D.Marcombe, *The Saint and the Swan. The Life and Times of St. Hugh of Lincoln*, Lincoln Cathedral Publications, 2000.

T.May, *An Economic and Social History of Britain 1760 – 1970*, Longman, 1987.

A.Mitchell and A.Tate, *Fishermen*, Hutton Press, 1997.

D.Mountfield, *Stage and Mail Coaches*, Shire, 2003.

C.Nicklin, *Trawling with the Lid Off*, Aurora Publishing, 1996.

M.Osborne, *Defending Lincolnshire*, The History Press, 2010.

R.I.Page, *Chronicles of the Vikings*, British Museum Press, 1995.

C.K.Rawding, *The Lincolnshire Wolds in the Nineteenth Century*, History of Lincolnshire Committee, 2001.

S.Richards, *Grand Old Ladies*, Archive publ. in assoc. with Grimsby Evening Telegraph, 1990.

D.N.Robinson, *The Lincolnshire Wolds*, Windgather Press, 2009.

J.Simpson, *The Viking World*, Batsford, 1980.

H.Thorold, *Lincolnshire Churches Revisited*, Michael Russell Ltd., 1989.

O.Thorsson, (Gen. Ed.) *The Sagas of the Icelanders*, Allen Lane The Penguin Press, 2000.

S.Toulson, *The Drovers*, Shire, 1980.

R.Wailes, *Lincolnshire Windmills (part I and II),* Newcomen Society, 1953,1955.

M.Watts, *Windmills,* Shire, 2006.

M.Watts, *Corn Milling*, Shire, 1983.

M.Watts, *Water and Wind Power*, Shire, 2000.

V.Willoughby, *The Errand Boy Who Went to Sea*, Richard Kay Publications, 1999.

G.Willson, ed., Recollections of a Lincolnshire Miller, *Louth Naturalists, Antiquarian and Literary Soc.,* 1994.

G.N.Wright, *Turnpike Roads*, Shire, 1992.

S.Yorke, *Windmills and Watermills Explained*, Countryside Books, 2006.

Websites

www.wales.ac.uk/en/CentreforAdvancedWelshCelticStudies

H.Griffith, *The Gremlin Question*, RAF Journal, 1942, at
www.angelfire.com/id/100sqn/gremlins.html

http:Penelope.uchicago.edu/Thayer/E/Gazeteer/Places/Europe/Gr
eat_Britain/England/_Topics/churches/Text/KINCAT*/home.html

Museums

East Kirkby Aviation Heritage Museum

Fishing Heritage Centre, Grimsby

Battle of Britain Memorial Flight Visitors' Centre, RAF
Coningsby

Museum of Lincolnshire Life, Lincoln

Hoyle's Mill, Alford

Ellis' Mill, Lincoln

Maps

Ordnance Survey Landranger Nos. 112, 113, 121, 122, 131

Ordnance Survey Explorer Nos. 261, 272, 281, 283, 284